CELEBRITY YEARBOOK

by Dan Carlinsky

PRICE/STERN/SLOAN
Publishers, Inc., Los Angeles
1983

Other Price/Stern/Sloan books by Dan Carlinsky:

ARE YOU COMPATIBLE?
DO YOU KNOW YOUR BOSS?
DO YOU KNOW YOUR HUSBAND?
DO YOU KNOW YOUR WIFE?
DO YOU KNOW YOUR PARENTS?

Copyright© 1982 by Carlinsky & Carlinsky, Inc.
Published by Price/Stern/Sloan Publishers, Inc.
410 North La Cienega Boulevard, Los Angeles, California 90048

ISBN: 0-8431-0619-0
Library of Congress Catalog Card Number: 82-61644

Introduction

Celebrities are just like you and your next-door neighbor. They put on their shirts one sleeve at a time exactly like the rest of us. They're just better known, that's all.

Leaf through this collection of old yearbook pictures of kids who grew up to be famous. Don't they look like you and your classmates looked in your school annual?

Sure they do. And if you focus on the faces one by one, you'll feel as though you're looking at old pictures of friends. Many of them you'll recognize in an instant; others, even with the clues given, you won't quite place. Some of us change more than others. Even celebrities.

I started collecting these photos–from schools, libraries, relatives and friends of the famous–some fifteen years ago. The task was challenging, and to the many who tried to make it a little easier I say thanks.

Over the years as each new picture arrived, I promptly tested it on anyone around. "Who's this?" I would ask, blocking the name of the celebrity. The universal oohs and ahs and wait-a-minute-don't-tell-me's convinced me this would be an enjoyable book.

I hope you'll agree.

Dan Carlinsky

If you should need them, answers can be found on pages 94 and 95.

BROOKVILLE HIGH '50
LYNCHBURG, VIRGINIA

☐☐☐☐☐ ☐☐☐☐☐☐

Football; baseball; basketball; editor-in-chief, BEE LINE.
"His head is full of just what it takes, _____ _____ should get all the breaks."

WHEATON COLLEGE '44
WHEATON, ILLINOIS

Anthropology major; president, Christian Council; Foreign Missionary Fellowship.

CENTRAL HIGH '30
MINNEAPOLIS, MINNESOTA

☐☐☐☐ ☐☐☐☐☐☐☐

Editor-in-chief, NEWS STAFF; president, Quill and Scroll; president, student council; Footlights; swimming; Class Cabinet.
"A purpose true, determined will; Pep, ability, and skill."

UNIVERSITY OF
NORTH CAROLINA '55
CHAPEL HILL, NORTH CAROLINA

☐☐☐☐☐☐☐ ☐☐☐☐☐

History major; Phi Eta Sigma; St. Anthony Hall fraternity; editor, DAILY TAR HEEL; Golden Fleece; Grail; Order of the Old Well; Publications Union Board; Graham Memorial Board of Directors; Orientation Counselor; Amphoterothen.

THE McCALLIE SCHOOL '43
CHATTANOOGA, TENNESSEE

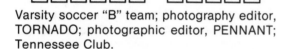

Varsity soccer "B" team; photography editor, TORNADO; photographic editor, PENNANT; Tennessee Club.

STAUNTON MILITARY ACADEMY '28
STAUNTON, VIRGINIA

☐☐☐☐☐ ☐☐☐☐☐☐☐☐☐

Monogram Club; Cotillion Club; Honor Committee; Officers Club; business manager, KABLEGRAM; staff, BLUE AND GOLD (yearbook); treasurer, senior class; company commander, "C" company; captain, swimming team; varsity basketball; varsity track; varsity football, All-State; Kable Legion of Honor (for "best all-around" cadet, school's highest award); nickname: "Goldberg."

JUNIOR PROM SYLLABUS QUEEN, Northwestern University

☐☐☐☐☐☐☐ ☐☐☐☐

BIRMINGHAM HIGH '65
VAN NUYS, CALIFORNIA

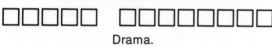

Drama.

WALTON HIGH '61
BRONX, NEW YORK

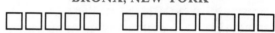

Volunteer aide; home room vice president; aide for Miss Chambers; aide for Mr. Fitzpatrick; ambition: secretary.

BEVERLY HILLS HIGH '61
BEVERLY HILLS, CALIFORNIA

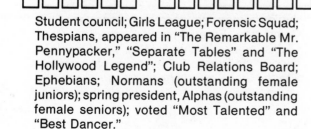

Student council; Girls League; Forensic Squad; Thespians, appeared in "The Remarkable Mr. Pennypacker," "Separate Tables" and "The Hollywood Legend"; Club Relations Board; Ephebians; Normans (outstanding female juniors); spring president, Alphas (outstanding female seniors); voted "Most Talented" and "Best Dancer."

**AMERICAN ACADEMY
OF DRAMATIC ARTS '56**
NEW YORK, NEW YORK

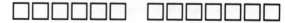

AMERICAN ACADEMY
OF DRAMATIC ARTS '29
NEW YORK, NEW YORK

☐☐☐☐☐ ☐☐☐☐☐☐☐☐☐

Played role of Mrs. Wynton in "The Last of Mrs. Cheyney."

SAN DIEGO HIGH '33
SAN DIEGO, CALIFORNIA

☐☐☐☐☐☐☐ ☐☐☐☐

Advanced Glee; Boys' Hi Jinx; Class B football; interclass football; interclass baseball; future: to attend state university.

KENYON COLLEGE '49
GAMBIER, OHIO

☐☐☐☐ ☐☐☐☐☐☐

Economics and drama majors; football; ran student laundry.
"Perennial T-barracks master of ceremonies, itinerant laundryman, antagonist of roommates and proctors alike, author of musical review, leading actor in dramatic productions, host to innumerable parties and never one to miss the opportunity for a fast buck are just a few of _____'s endearing charms."

GREENVILLE SENIOR HIGH '47
GREENVILLE, SOUTH CAROLINA

☐☐☐☐☐☐ ☐☐☐☐☐☐☐☐☐

Junior home room secretary; Secretary Club Committee; Entertainment Committee; Glee Club;appeared in "Junior Miss," Abe Lincoln in Illinois," "In Time to Come," "Joan of Lorraine."
"On the stage or off she was unsurpassed."

HAWTHORNE HIGH '60
HAWTHORNE, CALIFORNIA

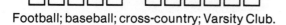

Football; baseball; cross-country; Varsity Club.

FREEHOLD HIGH '67
FREEHOLD, NEW JERSEY

College prep course.

L.C. HUMES HIGH '53
MEMPHIS, TENNESSEE

Shop, history and English majors; ROTC; Biology Club; English Club; History Club; Speech Club.

Last Will and Testament: "Donald Williams, Raymond McCraig and _____ leave hoping there will be someone to take their place as 'teachers' pets'?????"

Class Prophecy: "We are reminded at this time not to forget to invite you all out to the Silver Horse on Onion Avenue to hear the singing hillbillies of the road. _____, Albert Teague, Doris Wilburn and Mary Ann Propst are doing a bit of picking and singing out that-a-way."

IMMACULATE HEART HIGH '55
LOS ANGELES, CALIFORNIA

"The world is always ready to receive talent with open arms."

DANVILLE HIGH '44
DANVILLE, ILLINOIS

Vice president, Dramatic Club; student council; A Cappella Choir; Euterpean Singers; junior class president.

BEVERLY HILLS HIGH '62
BEVERLY HILLS, CALIFORNIA

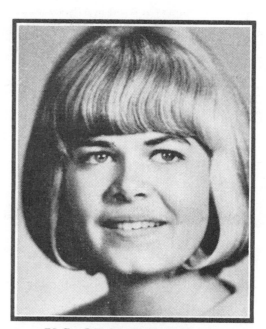

U.S. GRANT HIGH '65
PORTLAND, OREGON

President, Girls' League; cheerleader; Thespians; art award; Gendrills; honor girl; track; part-time jobs: waitress, drugstore clerk; chosen Football Court Princess; goal: undecided.

WEST VIRGINIA UNIVERSITY '48
MORGANTOWN, WEST VIRGINIA

Officer, Phi Sigma Kappa fraternity; appeared in University Theatre productions.

PHOENIX UNION HIGH '41
PHOENIX, ARIZONA

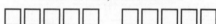

Spotlighters Club; staff, PHOENICIAN; staff, COYOTE JOURNAL (editor of April Fool's issue).

AMERICAN ACADEMY
OF DRAMATIC ARTS '47
NEW YORK, NEW YORK

JUST A GIRL NAMED JAYNE
St. Margaret's-McTernan School (Waterbury, Conn.

34

LOUISIANA STATE
UNIVERSITY '60
BATON ROUGE, LOUISIANA

☐☐☐ ☐☐☐☐

Journalism major; editor, DELTA (student literary annual).

GREAT NECK
NORTH SENIOR HIGH '56
GREAT NECK, NEW YORK

☐☐☐☐☐☐☐ ☐☐☐☐ ☐☐☐☐☐☐☐

"Francie"; band; Junior Players.

UNIVERSITY OF ILLINOIS '49
CHAMPAIGN, ILLINOIS

☐☐☐☐ ☐☐☐☐☐☐

Phi Eta Sigma (freshman honorary); freshman Honors Day; Granada Club (housing group); Chi Gamma Iota (veterans' rights and privileges); Psi Chi (psychology club); Phi Alpha Chi; Phi Alpha Delta (law club); Tomahawk (independent studies); Peterson Club; orchestra; appeared in "Mirth of a Nation"; sports editor.

THE AMERICAN UNIVERSITY '55
WASHINGTON,
DISTRICT OF COLUMBIA

☐☐☐☐☐☐☐ ☐☐☐☐☐

Philosophy and religion major; senior class Treasurer; Alpha Sigma Phi; job: announcer, local NBC radio station.

UNIVERSITY OF TEXAS '39
AUSTIN, TEXAS

□□□□ □ □□□□□□□□

President, Students' Association; dean, Delta Theta Phi (legal fraternity); Curtain Club; board member, Texas Union; board of directors, Texas Student Publications; debate society; Interfraternity Council; Round-Up Committee.

UNIVERSITY OF WASHINGTON
SCHOOL OF LAW '35
SEATTLE, WASHINGTON

□□□□□ □□□□□□□

Delta Chi; Phi Delta Chi; junior basketball manager.

ST. IGNATIUS COLLEGE
PREPARATORY '55
SAN FRANCISCO, CALIFORNIA

□□□□□ □□□□□

Freshman elocution and sophomore oratorical contest winner; Silver and Gold Medal debates; president, debating club; degree of distinction, National Forensic League competition; Christian Student Fellowship; Activities Dance Committee.

BATES COLLEGE '36
LEWISTON, MAINE

□□□□□□ □□□□□□

History and government majors; president, junior and senior class; vice president, Student Council; Debating Council; Politics Club; freshman track; Ivy Day speaker; honor work in government; Delta Sigma Rho; Phi Beta Kappa; voted "Most Respectable," "Best Scholar," "Most Likely to Succeed."
"Kings are not born; they are made by universal hallucination."

UNIVERSITY OF
SOUTHERN CALIFORNIA '37
LOS ANGELES, CALIFORNIA

☐☐☐ ☐☐☐☐☐

Merchandising major; teaching credits; jobs: cafeteria worker, library assistant, switchboard operator, department store clerk, bit movie actress; graduated cum laude.

WHITTIER HIGH '30
WHITTIER, CALIFORNIA

☐☐☐☐☐☐☐ ☐☐☐☐☐

Transfer from Fullerton High; scholarship; Latin Club; general manager of student body; president, Scholarship Society; features staff, CARDINAL & WHITE (newspaper); first prize in extemporaneous speaking (received $10 from Whittier Kiwanis Club, $20 from the Los Angeles Times); second place in district oratorical contest.

The Constitutional Oratorical Contest introduced a new feature this year, that of extemporaneous speaking. First Prize winner _____, of Whittier High (Cal.), spoke on "American Progress, Its Dependence Upon the Constitution."

AMERICA'S PROGRESS - ITS DEPENDENCE
UPON THE CONSTITUTION
BY _____ _____

. . . Fellow citizens, we have seen that without question the Constitution has been the underlying force in America's progress. We know that our forefathers have championed this document to the extent of giving their lives that we might enjoy its benefits. Yet in view of these facts, at the present time, a great wave of indifference to the Constitution's authority, disrespect of its law, and opposition to its basic principles threaten its very foundations. Shall we of the present generation allow this instrument to be cast into disrepute? Shall we be responsible for its downfall? If the nation wishes its progress to continue, this wave of indifference to the laws of the Constitution must cease . . .

NEW TRIER HIGH '59
WINNETKA, ILLINOIS

☐☐☐ – ☐☐☐☐☐☐☐
Senior show; cheerleader.

BEVERLY HILLS HIGH '52
BEVERLY HILLS, CALIFORNIA

☐☐☐☐☐☐☐ ☐☐☐☐☐☐☐☐☐☐
Chief Justice.

Cruising through the halls at
Kenyon College (O.)
☐☐☐☐ ☐☐☐☐☐☐

BERNARDS HIGH '67
BERNARDSVILLE, NEW JERSEY

☐☐☐☐☐ ☐☐☐☐☐☐
Gymnastics Club; French Club; varsity cheer-
leader; president, chorus; freshman class trea-
surer; Crimson; art editor, BERNARDIAN;
morning announcer; vice-president, Quill &
Scroll; Girls' State; swimming; school plays;
Prom Committee; National Honor Society;
chosen Homecoming Queen.
*"Pretty blonde; vivacious cheerleader; our
Homecoming Queen; many talents."*

51

SCHENLEY HIGH '45
PITTSBURGH, PENNSYLVANIA

Home Room Sec. 205.
"As genuine as a finger print."

UNIVERSITY OF MICHIGAN '39
ANN ARBOR, MICHIGAN

Track; Finance Committee; chairman of play production, Men's Union (which put on annual all-male show, the Union Opera).

AMERICAN ACADEMY OF DRAMATIC ARTS '50
NEW YORK, NEW YORK

Played role of Seth Lord in "The Philadelphia Story."

DENTON SENIOR HIGH '67
DENTON, TEXAS

Student Council; cheerleader; vice president, junior class; National Thespian Society; "Valentine Sweetheart"; Homecoming Queen nominee; "Miss D.H.S." (highest popularity honor).

BLUME HIGH '47
WAPAKONETA, OHIO

☐☐☐☐ ☐☐☐☐☐☐☐☐☐

Baritone horn player, band; yearbook staff; vice president, Student Council; Hi-Y; Boosters Club; junior year home room president; Boys' State; class play; Boy Scouts; flying lessons. *"He thinks, he acts, 'tis done."*

MARQUETTE UNIVERSITY
LAW SCHOOL '35
MILWAUKEE, WISCONSIN

CLEMSON UNIVERSITY '23
CLEMSON, SOUTH CAROLINA

☐☐☐☐☐ ☐☐☐☐☐☐☐☐

Horticulture major; president, Calhoun Literary Society; president, Edgefield-McCormick County Club; Agricultural Society; track; cross-country; baseball; basketball; football; ROTC. *"One cannot always be a hero, but one can always be a man."*

DARTMOUTH COLLEGE '30
HANOVER, NEW HAMPSHIRE

☐☐☐☐☐☐ ☐☐☐☐☐☐☐☐☐☐☐

Economics major; Casque and Gauntlet; Phi Beta Kappa; soccer; editor, THE FIVE LIVELY ARTS; class vice president; skiing; Sunday School teacher; spent senior year abroad, on fellowship studying music, painting, sculpture, architecture and photography in India and elsewhere.

Candidate for DARLING OF L.S.U.
Louisiana State University
☐☐☐☐☐☐ ☐☐☐☐☐☐☐

IT'S MAGIC!
Danville High (Ill.)
☐☐☐☐ ☐☐☐ ☐☐☐☐

PRESIDENT OF THE DEBATING CLUB
St. Ignatius College Prep (San Francisco, Cal.)
☐☐☐☐☐ ☐☐☐☐☐

GOING TO THE TOP
U.S. Military Academy (West Point, N.Y.)
☐☐☐☐☐☐ ☐
☐☐☐☐☐☐☐☐☐

LOOKING FOR AN OPEN COURT
Archbishop Molloy High (Briarwood, N.Y.)

☐☐☐☐☐ ☐☐☐☐☐☐☐☐☐

BARNARD COLLEGE '23
NEW YORK, NEW YORK

☐☐☐☐☐☐☐ ☐☐☐☐

Anthropology major; intercollegiate debating; editorial staff, BARNARD BULLETIN (newspaper); Phi Beta Kappa.
*"Economics, social science, _____
_____ has advanced ideas!"*

MILLBROOK SCHOOL '43
MILLBROOK, NEW YORK

☐☐☐☐☐☐☐ ☐ ☐☐☐☐☐☐☐

Football; newspaper staff; glee club; orchestra; co-editor, yearbook; honor roll; graduated summa cum laude.

UNIVERSITY OF
NORTH CAROLINA '17
CHAPEL HILL, NORTH CAROLINA

☐☐☐☐☐☐ ☐ ☐☐☐☐☐

Colonial Dames first prize; assistant editor, MAGAZINE; class historian; president, International Policy Club; class vice president; Commencement marshal; secretary, Greater Council; manager, Commencement Ball; vice president, Junior Law; Di Society; YMCA; Burke County Club; Dynamo; German Club; Mu Delta Phi; Sigma Upsilon.

THE GILBERT SCHOOL '51
WINSTED, CONNECTICUT

☐☐☐☐☐ ☐☐☐☐☐

Dramatic Club; scholarship.
"Anything for peace."
"Quiet; smart; can be found either at home or at the restaurant; woman hater."

SPORTS

YOU GOTTA BE
A FOOTBALL HERO

FROM A BIG KICK TO COACHING IN THE N.F.L.
UNIVERSITY OF TEXAS

GRIDIRON GREATS

A MAJOR REASON FOR VICTORY

EASTERN KENTUCKY UNIVERSITY

LEADING THE CHEERS
HURON HIGH (S.D.)

ONE OF "THE BOYS"
HAWTHORNE HIGH (CAL.)

□□
□□□□□□□

ED IS ON THE BALL
WYANDOTTE HIGH (KANSAS CITY, KAN.)

CENTER AND MOST VALUABLE PLAYER
UNIVERSITY OF MICHIGAN

□□□□□□ □□□□

GRIDIRON GREATS

CONGRATULATIONS, BUDDY, ON BEING NAMED
ALL-FLORIDA AND ALL-SOUTHERN
FLORIDA STATE UNIVERSITY

□□□□ □□□□□□□

A REAL TEAM PLAYER
WHITTIER COLLEGE

□□□□□□□ □□□□□

HOOPSTER HEROES
A Tisket, A Tasket, A Championship Basket

HE CAN DO IT ALL
NEWTOWN HIGH (CONN.)

☐☐☐☐☐ ☐☐☐☐☐☐

DAVID IS READY TO WIN
FAIRFAX HIGH
(LOS ANGELES, CAL.)

☐☐☐☐☐ ☐☐☐☐☐☐

PLAYING LIKE A REBEL WITHOUT A CAUSE
FAIRMOUNT HIGH (IND.)

☐☐☐☐☐ ☐☐☐☐

WITH HIS DANCE BAND
DUQUESNE UNIVERSITY

☐☐☐☐☐ ☐☐☐☐☐☐

KEEPING THE BEAT
SOUTHERN ILLINOIS UNIVERSITY

"OH ROCKET" OF
DANVILLE HIGH (ILL.)

☐☐☐☐☐ ☐☐☐☐☐

STUDENT BODIES

DESTINED TO BECOME A STAR
NEW TRIER HIGH (WINNETKA, ILL.)

□□□□ □□□□□□

ACTING THE PART OF A STUDENT
NEW TRIER HIGH (WINNETKA, ILL.)

□□□□□ □□□□

A REAL COMEDIAN
LOYOLA UNIVERSITY (ILL.)

□□□ □□□□□□□

AN ACTOR WHO WAS A MAGICIAN AND MUSICIAN
BUCKINGHAM BROWNE & NICHOLS SCHOOL (CAMBRIDGE, MASS.)

⬜⬜⬜⬜⬜⬜⬜ ⬜⬜⬜⬜⬜⬜

FROM THE FOOTBALL FIELD TO STAGE AND SCREEN
ABRAHAM CLARK HIGH (ROSELLE, N.J.)

⬜⬜⬜⬜⬜⬜⬜⬜⬜ ⬜⬜⬜⬜⬜

... AND GUESS WHO REMEMBERED HIS
CAP BUT FORGOT HIS GOWN?
BARD COLLEGE

□□□□□ □□□□□